Missing Pieces

Jennifer Maccar

Copyright © 2024 by Jennifer Maccar

All rights reserved.

No portion of this book may be reproduced in any form without written permission from the publisher or author, except as permitted by U.S. copyright law.

Contents

1. Meet the Addams ... 1
2. First Day of School and Discovering Them ... 3
3. Getting to Know Them and Learning The Addams Secret ... 7
4. Crumbled Fairytales ... 10
5. Unlocking Myself and Depression ... 13
6. Bella and danger go hand-in-hand ... 16
7. Uncovering the Truth ... 19
8. Italy, the Volturi, and Edward ... 22
9. Meeting the Cullens and Discussing Us ... 27
10. Introducing the Girlfriend and Boyfriend ... 31
11. Officially Meeting Mr. Swan ... 35
12. Florida, Here We Come! ... 37
13. Victoria and Powers ... 39
14. Missing Things, A Bonfire, and Wednesday Addams ... 43
15. Pain, Graduation, and Danger ... 47

16.	Gifts, Plans, and Engagements	52
17.	The Fight, Bree, and Saving them	55
18.	Pugsley's Happiness	58
19.	Getting Married to Forever	60
20.	Honeymoon: Night 1	63
21.	Honeymoon: Unexpected Results	66
22.	Pregnancy and Labor	68
23.	Babies, Transformations, and Death?!	71
24.	I'm Coming Home	73
25.	Panic Room	75
26.	Meet the Frumps	78
27.	Not Feeling Myself	79

Meet the Addams

First, we have the eldest of the family, Grandmama Eudora Addams. She is my father and Uncle Fester's mother. She is a witch. (though Calista doesn't know this yet) She lives with us.

Next, we have my Uncle Fester. He is my father's brother. Once he went missing in the Bermuda Triangle. Another time, our nanny married him and tried to kill him, but my baby brother saved us all. He loves cannons and can conduct electricity. He lives with us.

We also have Cousin Itt. He is extremely hairy. He is married to a woman named Margaret and they have a child named What. While they don't live with us, they do come to visit.

We also have Thing. He is a hand, that lives with us and works for us. Close friends with Lurch.

We have a butler named Lurch. My siblings and I treat him as family, as he helped raise us. He is one of my sister's best friends. Close friends with Thing.

The Patriarch of the family, my father, Gomez Addams. Some would refer to him as a Latinx Romeo. He is French and Hispanic.

The Matriarch, my mother, Morticia. The pale goddess.

My younger brother, Pugsley. He is 16. Watch out for his mischief, a street sign missing? Probably him. An Addams that doesn't have black hair, but a reddish blond.

My sister, Wednesday. She is 14. Watch out for her. She is much stronger than she looks and very dangerous. Best friends with Lurch and her doll, Marie Antoinette.

The youngest Addams was Pubert. The nanny had been for him and he saved us. Strangely, he disappeared after his first birthday. Maybe Cleopatra, my mother's plant, ate him?

Finally , we have me - Calista Ophelia Addams. I am 17 years old. I am the odd ball in the family. I don't look like my family. The Addams usually have black hair and dark colored eyes. I have ginger hair and blue eyes, sharing the hair color with Cousin Itt strangely. However, there is no doubt that I am an Addams and you will see why.

When You're An Addams!

First Day of School and Discovering Them

The first day at a new school is always hard, but it's always harder when the school is in a tiny town. Calista Addams had moved to Forks, Washington with her parents and younger siblings. Forks High School rarely received new student, yet, she was the second new Senior in six months. It was a month into the school year, the date being September 9th.

Calista lowered her head, staring at her boots as she walked down the hall. She could feel all the eyes staring at her, judging her and watching her every action. Caught up in her thoughts, she didn't notice where she was going. Next thing she knew, she was hovering over a girl on the ground. As she looked at her, the heart within her chest seemed to try to escape.

The girl beneath Calista was the most beautiful creature she had ever seen. Her hair a gorgeous, caramel brown that complemented her chocolate brown eyes. Her skin was as pale as that of an Addams. The girl moved a bit and snapped her out of her trance. She rose to her feet and helped the beauty to hers.

"I- I'm so sorry. I wasn't paying attention! Are you ok?!," Calista spluttered out, beginning to bite her bottom lip. She then heard a sexy chuckle, causing her to look up. Behind the beautiful girl was a handsome male. His hair was a bronze and his eyes were an outstanding topaz color. He was even paler than the Addams family! She felt the same reaction as when she looked at the girl.

She blushed before looking down at the floor. "It was my fault too; I am too clumsy! You must be new; we've never seen you before. My name is Bella Swan and this is my boyfriend, Edward Cullen.," the girl, Bella, told her. Her boyfriend nodded, the girl before them would have been very hard to miss. She was beautiful, her skin matching the color of Bella's and her ginger hair setting off her blue eyes.

For some reason, the name Cullen sounded familiar to her. She would have to ask her parents when she returned home. When Bella said they were dating, Calista's heart broke in half. "I- I- I'm Calista Addams. I moved her with my parents and younger siblings. I have to go to the office.," she told them before walking away, her heart aching. What was she feeling?!

Calista entered the office and received her schedule. Almost as if her body had wasn't hers, she ran out of the school and jumped into her car. On autopilot, she drove herself home before running into the forest. When she regained control of herself, she was at the edge of a cliff. Unable to contain herself, she dropped to the ground and sobbed began to rack her body.

An Addams rarely cried! Then again, Calista wasn't an ordinary Addams. She had met these two beautiful people and already they had control over her. Was this love? It reminded her of the way her parents acted together. These two had stolen her heart at first sight and caused it to crumble.

When her cries had subsided, Calista pulled herself up from the forest floor. She didn't know where she was or which way she had come from. She began to wander the forest, looking for the way out and the way home. When she finally made it home, it was around six P.M.! Her parents bombarding her with questions as soon as she entered.

"Calista Ophelia Addams! Where have you been?! The school called saying that you grabbed your schedule and took off from the school. Wait... are you alright, My Love?!," her parents spouted at her. She shook her head, before they enveloped her in a hug. They held her close as she began to sob once more.

"It hurts so much! I walked into the school and ended up falling on top of a girl. She was so beautiful, my heart tried to escape its cage. When I helped her up, there was a handsome guy behind her. My heart doubled its efforts at the sight of them together.

"The two of them were dating! This shattered my heart and I couldn't take it. I grabbed the schedule and hopped in my car. I dropped the car off here and took off into the forest. I broke down on the forest floor, crying for hours. Then it finally stopped, I discovered I got lost and tried to find the way out. If this is love, please take it away!!," Calista explained to her parents, clutching her chest in pain.

"My Love, I think so. Your heart always did have enough room for more than one person. I'm sorry, perhaps they will accept you into their relationship? We will let you take the day off from school on Monday.," Morticia told her daughter. Calista nodded and wiped her tears away.

"The boy's last name sounded so familiar to me. Do we know any Cullens?," Calista asks her parents, before describing the couple to them. "His skin is even paler than ours, with her skin being our color. Her beautiful caramel locks looked exquisite next to his bronze hair. His eyes a beautiful Topaz and hers a yummy chocolate brown."

"Cullen? We did know one. Ask him who his father is when you see him next. They do sound very attractive. What was her name, Dear Heart?,"

Gomez asked. They had never seen Calista so happy. When she talked about the couple, her eyes got a far away look and she smiled. "Her name is Bella Swan and his first name is Edward. She moved here six months ago to live with her father. He is the Chief of Police here in Forks.," She explained to her father.

Getting to Know Them and Learning The Addams Secret

When Calista returns to school on the 13th, She immediately looks for Edward and Bella. When she spots them, they are talking to a small, pixie like girl and a boy who looked pained. She pause in her approach. She heard the bell-like voice wish Bella a happy birthday and that she would see her tonight. The girl received a shushing and a 'do I have to?' from Bella, making her chuckle . It was her birthday?!, she wished had known.

Bella spotted Calista and rushed over to her with Edward by her side. "What happened, Calista?! You disappeared after talking to us and the whole school went into a frenzy. Are you okay?," Bella asked, she felt happier when the girl was with her and Edward. This caused her to blush; she didn't mean to send the school into absolute chaos.

" I-I had a slight anxiety attack and panic took over. After grabbing my schedule, my body went into autopilot and I left the school. I drove my car home and then ran into the forest. When the attack subsided, I realized that I had no idea where I was and tried to find the way home. I reached home at like 6 P.M. My parents let me take yesterday off to recover.," Calista explained.

"Did that girl say today was your birthday, Bella? Happy Birthday! 18?," Calista whispered, knowing she didn't want it publicized. Bella blushed, flattered that she had acknowledged that she didn't want it said. Calista remembered what her father had told her to ask. "Edward, what is your father's name? My parents recognized the name Cullen. They thought that there might be a connection.," she asked him.

"Carlisle is my father's name. He is a doctor at the Forks Community Hospital. Maybe they do have a connection.," Edward told Calista, doubting that her parents knew anyone related to Carlisle. She thanked him and asked if she could have their numbers. They agreed and before she knew it, the school day was over.. She drove home and put way her backpack.

Calista headed to the study, where her parents sat snuggled up at the desk. "Edward told me his father's name today. His name is Carlisle and he is a doctor at the hospital in town. Does it sound familiar?," She asked as she saw the look her parents shared. It was about time she learned the truth about them anyway. "Yes, that's the name of the Cullen we knew. But we knew a Carlisle back in 1911. There is something we need to tell you. Your Grandmama is a witch and so is your Granny Frump. They gave us potions to slow down our aging process.", Gomez told his eldest daughter.

Calista gave them a deadpan look and let out a little chuckle. "Very funny. You definitely weren't alive in 1911! My grandmothers aren't witches.," She replied to her parents, who called for Grandmama. "Are you in on this too, Grammy? Are you going to say that you are a witch? I know we aren't exactly normal, but we are humans. Wait... What are you doing?," She asked as Grandmama pulled out a small vial with silvery liquid inside.

"Child, you need to hush or I will turn you into a toad! I am a witch and so is Granny Frump, we went to school together. Drink this or I will make you drink it.," Grandmama snapped at her. Calista grabbed the vial and drank it, before feeling like she needed to sleep. She heard her grandmother mutter, "And to think this is the next Addams witch.". Calista was soon lost to the world for the next three days, as her body slumped forward and thudded to the floor.

Crumbled Fairytales

Calista woke up on the night of the 16th at around 9 P.M., her phone was ringing and caller ID said it was Bella. "Hello?," she answered. But, the voice on the other end wasn't her. "This is her father, Charlie. I called to see if you know where Bella is. She has called and texted you a lot over the last three days, so I thought she could be with you.," Charlie told her.

"No, Bella isn't here. I thought you were her... She's missing?!! Hold on, give me your address and I will come help look for her.," Calista told him, panicking about Bella. Charlie gave her the address and hung up. Wait... three days? She checked her phone, the date displaying as September 16th. She had been asleep for three whole days!! Her phone displayed at least 50 texts from Bella and 10 missed calls.

Calista grabbed a coat before running out the door. She hopped into her car and sped to the address Charlie had given her. When he had hung up the phone, he had discovered a note saying that Bella had gone into the woods with Edward. She ran into the woods, ignoring as the tree branches cut at her face. Soon, she lost her footing and rolled down a slight incline. As she went, her legs and arms received lacerations, her right arm and left leg breaking as they hit a large rock and tree.

Her head slammed against boulder and her body hit another object. She managed to roll herself over and saw what she had hit as she heard whimpering. There beside her was Bella, curled up in a ball. She was whimpering and mumbling as she lay there shivering on the forest floor in her thin jacket. Calista removed her own coat and wrapped it around her, screaming for someone to come help. She wished she could do more.

Her scream reached the ears of two men from the Quileute tribe, who had been called to aid in the search for Bella. The men both had black hair, russet skin, and an identical tattoo on their upper right arm. They tell the girls that everything will be okay. One of them picking up Calista, who relishes in the unexpected yet welcomed warmth he gives off. The elder male carries Bella, who whimpers for Edward. When they begin to walk, Calista loses consciousness.

When she woke up, she found herself in a hospital room. She blinked as her eyes adjusted to the blinding white lights above. Calista tried to move, but didn't get far as her siblings grabbed her. Tear tracks could be seen on Wednesday's face and tears still streamed from Pugsley's eyes. Her sister never cried! What had happened?! She began to panic, her rate monitor spiking rapidly.

"Pugsley, get mother and father. Calista, everything is going to be ok. You got hurt.," Wednesday explained to her sister. This caused what had happened to return to her. Her brother entered the room, followed by her parents and a doctor. "So, Miss Addams. Looks like you took quite a nasty tumble last night. You had quite a few injuries and as such need to be out of school for at least a week.," the doctor explained.

Stitches covered her arms and her right had a cast from the elbow down, having broken everything below it. Her legs were in the same condition, but her left leg had the cast from the knee down, completely shattered. Calista asked for a hand mirror to see what other damage had occurred.

She almost cried at the sight that awaited her. Her skin was marred with bruises, busted lips, broken nose, and many stitches all over.

The doctor provided the family with a wheelchair and released her. They transferred her into their car. "Are my necklaces ok? Wait.... Is Bella ok?!! ANSWER ME!!!," Calista asked, her voice rising to a shout at the end. They assured her that they would explain things when they arrived at home. Wednesday squeezed her sister's left hand, reassuring her that everything would be fine.

"Your necklaces are fine. Bella's unharmed, at least physically. Her father called to thank you for finding her and apologizing for you getting hurt. Emotionally, she's destroyed, due to Edward leaving her in the woods alone. She screams in her sleep as if someone is killing her. He wants to see if she will open up to you once you can walk again.," Morticia explained to her daughter. Calista began to sob uncontrollably. Half of her heart destroyed by the other half abandoning it, leaving her with a gaping and jagged hole.

Unlocking Myself and Depression

Before Calista knew it, a special day had come along. Her leg had healed enough for her to limp around in her cast because a month had past since the accident. Today was special because it was not only Halloween, but her 18th birthday. Grandmama told her that tonight her life would change forever and to be ready by 11 P.M. She had no idea what was planned.

Seeing as it was only 3 P.M., Calista decided to try and visit Bella. She got into her car and drove to the address she had saved. She knocked on the front door and Charlie answered. He let her in, but told her Bella wasn't doing any better. She still wanted to see here, even if it would be a one sided conversation. Last time she had seen her was the day it happened.

Charlie sighed, but decided that it couldn't hurt to try. Calista limped over to Bella's room and entered. Bella was staring out her window, unmoving and unnoticing of her presence. The sight caused the gaping hole in her chest to burn . "Hey, Bella. Today is my 18th birthday. My family told me that truths would be revealed to me on this day, but I wish I could take away your pain instead. I need you by my side.," Calista rambled, her voicing cracking and shaking as a tear threatened to fall. She stood and left after squeezing her shoulder.

"I'll be back again soon, Mr. Swan. It hurts to see her like this. It hurts so much.," she told him before leaving the house. She got into her car and drove herself home. Calista decided she needed to scream out her pain and ran upstairs to her room. She buried her face in a pillow and let it all out. When she couldn't manage to produce anymore, it was already 6 P.M.

The screams made her throat raw and sore, taking away a lot of her energy. Calista went downstairs and decided to make herself a steak and some juice. She loved her meat on the rare side, so it didn't take too long to cook. Once she had finished her meal, she became sleepy. A nap could help pass the time to 11.

When she fell asleep, Calista began to have nightmares. She dreamt of the night that she found Bella. But, this time she wasn't alive, but a lifeless corpse with dull eyes that followed her. The corpse asked her why she didn't save her, that no one loved her because all she brought was pain. She shot awake at 10 P.M., the nightmare causing her chest to burn .

She got up and dressed in the outfit her Grandmama had laid out for her to wear. She had specific instructions to not wear shoes and to do her makeup as told. Calista was to bring her blood vial necklace and head to the middle of the forest. This was a ritual to activate her witch powers! She looked in the library of the house earlier and discovered that they were magic.

The clock struck 10:55 and Calista began the trek to the specified location. She reached the spot at exactly 11, her Grandmama waiting for her there. She looked down at the forest floor, spotting a shape. There was a pentagram made of sticks and stones before her, which her grandmother gestured to. She stepped into the center and was told to sit cross-legged.

Calista was then instructed to open the blood vial and drink it. While she did, her grandmother began to chant a spell. The pentagram around her began to set ablaze, trapping her inside! she was then told to place her hands palm up and stare at the full moon above them. When she did as told, her body to glow a golden color and started to float.

She felt a sudden burning in the center of her back and the right side of her color bone to above her breast. But, as soon as the pain began, it dissipated and she was lowered to the ground. Calista passed out as the fiery pentagram put out itself out. Grandmama smiled down at her, she had finally unlocked her true self. She carried her granddaughter back to the house.

Bella and danger go hand-in-hand

It had been four and a half months since Calista had gotten to see Bella. She spent every day in pain, did she not like her anymore? Had she done something wrong? Charlie had told her that Bella didn't want to see her, even though she had come out of her depression back in January. Instead, she was hanging out with a younger boy in La Push, a Quileute named Jacob Black.

Today was the 16th of March, only the fourth day of Spring Break. Calista jumped into her car and decided to go visit La Push, where Charlie said Bella was. As she drove down a rocky road, she spotted a figure standing at the edge of a cliff. When she got closer, she felt as if she couldn't breath as she recognized them. It was Bella!!

She jumped out of the car and screamed out her name. Unfortunately, Bella didn't hear her until after she had leapt off. She looked back with a shocked face as she plummeted. Calista threw off her shoes and sped over to the cliff, jumping in after Bella. When she hit the water, a hand grabbed her ankle, dragging her deeper into the murky depths. As her lungs burned for air, she was soon forced to gasp, causing her lungs to fill with the cold water.

Calista's vision began to blur as her chest burned and ached. Her brain started to become fuzzy, causing her to fade in and out of consciousness. She thought of Bella and how she had failed to protect her. She thought of her family, knowing that she would never return to them. Right before she blacked out, Calista saw a figure dive into the water and grab the girl that stole half of her heart.

Jacob brought Bella to the beach and began to preform CPR on her, pushing the water out of her lungs. She sat up gasping, looking around and starting to panic. She had seen Calista jump in after her, so where was she. Jacob looked at her confused about her searching. "Where's Calista?! She jumped in after me. CALISTA?!!!," Bella screamed, stumbling around to look.

"Who's Calista? There wasn't anyone else in the water...," Jacob asked her. Soon, the sound of a splash reached their ears. Bella was the first to see the cause, screaming and running to the water. "NO!!! I shouldn't have ignored you. I should have told you how you made me feel. I was so scared. Please don't leave me too!! Jake, please help her.," Bella cried, cradling Calista against her chest. Jacob looked as she held the body of a pale girl with ginger hair.

He ran over to her and grabbed the motionless girl. He began chest compressions and gave her some mouth to mouth. Jacob also turned her head in an attempt to remove the water from her lungs. Soon, water was pouring out of Calista's mouth and her chest began to rise and fall. Her eyes opened into his and she began to panic.

Her panic soon ended as she spotted Bella. "What the hell was that Bella?! First, your father tells me you don't want to see me. Now, you try to kill yourself?!! I would be lost without you, Bella! You own half of my heart. What did I do to hurt you? Please take it out on me.," Calista cried.

"You didn't do anything. I didn't try to kill myself, I was cliff diving. I didn't want to accept what I felt about you, but seeing you lifeless destroyed me. You own half of my heart as well, but I still love HIM as well.," Bella told her. Calista smashed her lips against those of the beautiful girl before her.

What she felt was outstanding! Her lips tingled and fireworks erupted inside of her. Her hand raised and weaved itself into Bella's hair. Half of her heart mended itself within her chest, relieving half of the pain. Calista felt content in the kiss, until Jacob cleared his throat.

The two girl parted from the kiss and blushed at the fact he had seen it. He felt awkward, he still would try to get Bella to be his, but he felt as though he saw was meant to be. He told her that he was going to drive her to his house for some dry clothes and then take her home later. Calista told Bella that she would drop by once she sent her a text. She didn't know what awaited her at the Swan household.

Uncovering the Truth

Calista received a text from Bella a couple hours after changing clothes. She wanted to look pretty for Bella, hoping she would lose her. Arriving at the house, a strange car was outside and Jacob stood there rather tense. He smelled musky to her, but she thought nothing of it. He stopped her as she went toward the door. "Don't. It's not safe.," he told her, causing her eyes to widen.

"What do you mean it's not safe?! Bella is in there!!," Calista yelled at him. He sighed and opened the door for the both of them. Alice Cullen stood in the room, smelling sweet and floral. She rushed to Bella's side. "Jacob said it wasn't safe. Did she hurt you?! Also why do they both have strange smells?," she questioned.

"Jake is paranoid and no she would never hurt me, Calista. What do you mean they have strange smells?," Bella asked, smiling at the girl. Both girls blushed as they remembered the kiss they had shared. "He smells musky and she smells sweet and floral. Alice never smelled like this to me before...," she explained.

The others were surprised, only the supernatural could smell each other. But, as far as they knew, Calista was human. "Has anything happened to you recently, Calista?," Alice asked. How did she know that there was a change to her? "You probably won't believe me.... I changed on my 18th birthday. We held a ritual to unlock my witch powers. Both of my grandmothers are witches and I inherited the gene.," she explained.

Calista asked them to wait as she ran to car and grabbed her spare outfit. She put it on, it revealed her tattoos and marks. She walked into the room, receiving gasps. " The one on my back is my witches mark. I have a quote from my mother on my side. The one on my collarbone is called my mate mark.," Calista told them, blushing as she mentioned the last one.

"So that's how you can smell us... Only a supernatural can smell another.," Alice explained. She knew that Calista was the third piece to Bella and Edward's puzzle, but she hadn't seen her being a witch. "What are you then? My parents said they knew a Carlisle back in 1911. Is your father the same man? What is Jacob?," she rambled.

"Yes, I believe he is the same man, but we will have to ask him. As for what I am, a vampire. Jacob is a shapeshifter. He turns into an large wolf.," Alice told Calista, she couldn't believe how calm she was.

"Stoicism is an Addams trait, if you were wondering. I should have known if I exist, so would other beings. How should I trust either of you near Bella? I read that shifters are very volatile beings. Vampires drinking human blood.," Calista said, eyeing the two supernaturals.

"My family feeds off of animals only. Jasper is the newest to the diet, being the reason we left. Bella was injured at her birthday party, causing him to go into a frenzy. He didn't mean to, Bella.," Alice told them. Calista looked at Jacob, waiting for his explanation.

"I would never hurt Bella! We protect humans. We have been chasing the cause of the danger.," Jacob explained, eyes drawn to Calista's wrist. " A stupid red-haired bloodsucker. She jumped into the water around the same time Bella did."

Calista looked down at her wrist and saw what he was staring at. Her entire wrist was a deep purple color in the shape of a feminine hand. She realized that the vampire must have been the one to drag her through the murky depths. "I may have encountered her. Someone was dragging me further into the water after I jumped to save Bella.," she told them. She showed the other girls the bruise.

"I didn't see you jump in... But, I can't see past the mutts. I can see your future as well, Jacob must have interfered with it.," Alice told her, grabbing the wrist. Calista enjoyed the cold skin against the burning, but was confused by what she said. "Wait... Did you say see my future?!," she exclaimed. She received a nod and tried to ask if anyone else had abilities. But she was cut off by the phone ringing.

Jacob answered the phone with a quick hello. He listened to the other end before replying, "No. He's at the funeral." Calista's eyebrows furrowed, who was dead? Soon, Bella popped up and asked who that was. "It was Dr. Carlisle Cullen.," he told her. Alice ran out the door and soon returned saying one word, "Edward!"

Italy, the Volturi, and Edward

"Please don't go! Bella, stay for me. Stay for Charlie!," Jacob pleaded, trying to stop her. Alice had informed them of her vision about Edward. Rosalie had told him why she had returned to Forks, but she didn't know that Bella was still alive. Edward was distraught and planned to have the Volturi kill him. He didn't want to exist in a world without her.

When Calista heard, her chest began to burn. She couldn't lose him, not before she actually had him! Bella looked over at the girl, realizing that she too loved Edward. She loved her and him, in an equal manner. They had to get there in time. Alice smiled, they were on the track to becoming what she saw.

She purchased tickets for the three of them and they raced to the airport. Bella and Calista held onto one another, trying to keep the other from breaking apart. The later whispered, "What are we, Bell? What will become of us once Edward is back?" She feared they would leave her behind, a broken and bleeding mess.

"I love you, Calista. Would you be my girlfriend? We will take it a step at a time. I think he may feel the same way. Either way, we are now a package deal.," Bella told her. Calista nodded and pulled her into a deep kiss.

The plane took off on the 11-hour trip from Forks, Washington to Volterra, Italy. Alice looked over to the girls. Bella's head rested upon Calista's chest as they held each other. Both of them sound asleep. Right before the plane landed, she woke them up.

Alice ran off and returned with a flashy sports car. On the drive to the Volturi, she explained to them that Edward's request had been denied. He wasn't giving up, he was going to expose himself to the humans, forcing them to kill him. If she went to stop him, he wouldn't believe her claims. It had to be them.

Bella and Calista held hands as they raced toward the alcove that contained Edward. They couldn't lose him! As he started to emerge, the girls took a shortcut through a fountain. They leapt out and managed to reach him at the last moment. The girls collided into his exposed chest as it started to shine.

Edward smelled the familiar scents and opened his eyes. He looked down into his arms and spotted them. Bella was alive and Calista was with her. He buried his face into their hair, breathing in the scents. Soon, they separated and walking to an alley.

"Bella.... Why is Calista here?," Edward asks, concerned for their safety. Had she dragged her into this, endangered her? "Calista helped me when you left, she found me that day. She knows, Edward. She isn't exactly human....," Bella told him, biting her lip. She would leave it to the girl to explain herself.

"Bella's right. The day I met the two of you, my life changed. I no longer owned my heart. It was split between the two of you, breaking when you said you were dating. That's why I ran that day, scared at the control you held over me. On Bella's birthday, I decided to try to get to know you.

"I told my parents your father's name and the world turned upside down. They told me they had met a Carlisle Cullen back in 1911. That my grandmothers were witches and gave them potions to extend their lives. I didn't believe them, but then my Grandmama gave me a potion that sent me to sleep.," Calista told them, before pausing.

She took a deep breath, preparing herself for what was to come next. "I woke up at 9 P.M. on September 16th to a phone call from Charlie. He thought Bella might have been with me. She had called me 10 times and texted me 50 over the three days. I panicked and asked for their address. I went into the forest to look for her and eventually did.

"I ran through the trees, trying to find her and I tripped. My arms and legs received lacerations as I fell. My left leg wrapped around a tree and everything from the knee down broke. My right arm smashed into a large rock, causing everything below the elbow to shatter. Still I kept rolling, until my head slammed against a boulder and my body into Bella's. I called for help and we were soon rescued. I woke up in the hospital.," Calista explained, before pausing again.

Bella hugged her tight and Edward thanked her for finding the brunette. "When I could finally hobble around, it was my 18th birthday. I went to see Bella and wished I could celebrate with her. But there was a ritual planned that night. It unlocked my powers, giving me my mate mark and witches mark. I didn't get to see Bella again for four and a half months.

"Charlie told me she didn't want to see me and that she was hanging out in La Push. I had enough and decided to try and find her there. What awaited me was Bella standing on the edge of the cliff. I jumped after her, hoping to save the girl I loved. But a hand grabbed my wrist and started to drag me into the depths. Jacob saved her, but I drowned.," Calista said, shocking Edward.

He didn't know that she had jumped as well or that she loved him and Bella. How was she here if she drowned?!! "Bella freaked out when she couldn't find me and soon spotted me floating on the surface. She grabbed me and started to cry, begging Jacob to save me. He did and I chewed her out for jumping off the cliff. We ended up kissing, before heading to change into dry clothes.

"Bella texted me to tell me I could come over. I saw the strange car and went toward the door, only for Jacob to stop me. He smelled musky to me as he told me it wasn't safe. We entered the house wanted to protect her and Alice was there. She smelled sweet and floral, which I mentioned. I told them about me and they told me what they were. Jacob is a Shapeshifter.," Calista told Edward, stepping forward and hugging him.

She wanted to show him that she wasn't scared of him. But the hug was cut short as voices came up behind them. Two males with black hair and blood red eyes stared at them. They were dressed in black cloaks with red linings. A small girl arrived and told them that Aro wanted to see them, Edward reluctantly agreed. Calista could tell from his reaction that the girl was not to be messed with.

Alice joined them as they walked into the Volturi throne room. Three male vampires stood before them, while other vampires stood guard. The vampire looking similar to the female spoke, "Sister, they send you out for one and you bring back two... and two halves. Such a clever girl." Another vampire, one with long black hair and an air of authority, greets them. He tells them it is good that Bella is not dead after all. His gaze transfers to Calista, interested in her connection to the couple. She appeared human as well.

Danger soon unfolded as the Volturi tried to use their powers on Bella. It caused Calista to use her powers for the first time. Her hands glowed with a black flame as she growled at them. Alice soon stepped in and promised that the girls would become vampires. They were ushered out of the building and boarded the plane home.

A/N: please don't hate me for relating everything to Edward.... I hope you guys like it; I also wrote so much I didn't think I should describe everything with the Volturi. SORRY FOR THIS IF YOU ACTUALLY EVEN READ THIS STORY

Meeting the Cullens and Discussing Us

On the return flight to Forks, Edward decided to talk to Calista. "I have felt a connection to you since we met. Alice had a vision of you, me, and Bella together. Do you actually love us, Calista?," he asked. She nodded and asked if she could try something. Her hand caressed his marble skin, dancing her fingertips across his gorgeous lips. He did the same to her, before lifting her into his lap.

He lowered his head and connected their lips. Calista began to try and deepen the kiss, but Edward separated them. He told her he didn't want to hurt her. She pouted, but thought of the way the kiss had made her feel. Her heart was now complete and her lips tingled with fireworks. She leaned over to Bella and gave her a kiss as well.

"What does this make us? My heart couldn't take it if I lost either of you. Plus, when an Addams loves it is with their entire being. I don't think I could ever love anyone else. Bella had asked me to be her girlfriend on the plane ride to save you. But, Edward, do you want me?," Calista asked, blushing.

"Of course, love. Will you, Calista Addams, be my girlfriend? Will you make it into OUR girlfriend instead? I love you and Bella. Now that I have had a taste, I won't let go.," he asked, holding her hand.

"Yes. I am yours and Bella's girlfriend. You are my first boyfriend and girlfriend. I had never felt anything for anyone before the two of you. You are my fairytale ending.," Calista said, snuggling into the two of them.

She soon fell asleep on her partners, feeling the happier than she ever had before. Her dream was of the three of them getting married. Edward stood at the altar in a sexy tuxedo, Bella currently walking toward him in an elegant gown. The gown lacked any details, but she knew if her love wore it, anything would be beautiful. Soon it was her turn to walk to them.

Her dress was a dark, Victorian style gown. She couldn't make out anything about its actual appearance, but she didn't care. She walked down the aisle to the loves of her life. But, as she reached them, she pulled back to reality. Edward and Bella were shaking her shoulders to wake her. They had made it back to Forks.

"Alice is going to take you to your house, so you can change. Wear something special, I want you to meet my family.," Edward told Calista. She looked up at him shocked, he wants her to meet the rest of the Cullens?! Well, it was only fair, now that they were dating. She wondered how it would go when he met her family.

The ride back to the Addams house was quiet. Alice smiled at Calista, happy that she was now with Edward and Bella. They were finally completed and the family will love her. She had a much larger collection of clothes than Bella. They all balanced each other out, the perfect combination.

Calista jumped out when they arrived, speeding up to her room. She decided on a dress with heels and went to pick out some accessories. Eventually, she decided on her regular jewelry, adding gloves and headband. She hurried back to the car, throwing a quick 'we will talk when I get home' to her parents. After waiting for her to buckle in, Alice headed for the Cullen household.

When they arrived, Bella and Edward were sitting on the coach. He smiled when she came in, motioning her to sit with them. She looked beautiful, like a witchy goddess. Her girlfriend wrapped her arms around her waist and nibbled lightly on her neck. Calista looked at them as if they were the very air she needed to live.

"Who's this, Edward? She is very beautiful.," a woman with a heart shaped face asked. Calista thought she was gorgeous, her hair many different shades of brown. "This is Calista Addams, she is our girlfriend. She came with Bella to save me.," he explained, kissing the girl's cheek. She blushed, still not used to the attention. This was news to all the Cullens, except Alice.

"This is my mother, Esme. The man beside her is my father, Carlisle. Beside Alice is her husband, Jasper. The two near the wall are Emmett and his wife Rosalie.," Edward explained to her. She nodded before remembering that she had something to ask Carlisle.

"Carlisle, do you know a Morticia and Gomez Addams, from 1911?," Calista asked, looking at up at him. He began to think, looking back through his many memories. "Yes. He is a Latino and she is a very pale skinned woman?," he asked her, to which she nodded. She would tell them that he was the same man. "They are my parents.," she said, shocking the entire group.

How could that be possible?!! "I'll explain in the shortest way possible. I'm a witch, since my 18th birthday back on Halloween. The gene came from both of my grandmothers. My parents received potions from their mothers to slow down their aging. So, they have looked no older than 30 since then.," Calista told them.

The Cullens loved Calista. They couldn't have asked for a better person to complete Edward and Bella. She was beautiful and a kind soul. They knew that she would love the two of them forever. The two, in turn, would love her unconditionally always. "I can't wait to see how it goes when you two meet my parents. Bella, you will also have to reintroduce me to Charlie.," Calista said, giggling.

Introducing the Girlfriend and Boyfriend

Calista called her partners and told them to come over to meet her parents. She got dressed in an outfit that she knew they would love. It was still hard for her to believe that they chose her to be their girlfriend. When her mother texted her saying they were in the living room, her breath caught in her chest. Might as well give them an entrance they wouldn't be able to forget.

She turned on the song 'Straight to Hell' and sang along as she descended the grand staircase. As she came down, Bella and Edward stared at her in awe. Their girlfriend was drop dead gorgeous! Gomez and Morticia Addams watched their reaction to their eldest daughter. They loved her, never wanting to harm their beloved Calista.

She reached the bottom of the stairs and walked towards her loves. They pulled her between them on the couch, snuggling into her. Calista's face broke out into a huge smile as she blushed. "Mother, Father, I wanted to introduce you to the people that stole my heart. This is my girlfriend, Bella Swan and my boyfriend, Edward Cullen.", She told her parents.

"Edward's father is the Carlisle you met back in 1911. The Cullens are vampires. Bella is human, but has a freaking Shapeshifter best friend! His name is Jacob Black, living in La Push as a member of the Quileute tribe. He saved Bella's life and mine as well.," Calista told them.

"What do you mean he saved your life?!!," Morticia screamed, causing Gomez to pull her into his lap. She had been about to lunge herself at the three lovers. Calista rubbed the back of her neck, trying to figure out how to explain the situation. Short and sweet was most likely the best way. She grabbed her partners hands for comfort.

"Bella had been ignoring me after she came out of the depression, but I needed to see her. Her father, Charlie, told me that she was hanging out in La Push, so I went to find her. I found her on the edge of a cliff and called to her, but she had already jumped. Panicking, I launched myself in after her. A hand grabbed my wrist and started to drag me into the depths below.," Calista explained.

"As I thought the life left me, I saw a figure pull Bella out of the water. I blacked out and came to on the beach, her friend having given me CPR. Angry, I spilled everything about my feelings out to Bella and she returned them. We had our first kiss right there.," Calista said, blushing as she remembered it.

"I went back to her house after getting changed, but Jacob told me it wasn't safe. He had started to smell musky to me, and I began to freak out for Bella's safety. I got him to enter with me and Alice Cullen stood there. She is Edward's sister and I had met her before, but she smelled different. She gave off a sweet and floral scent, as I asked Bella if she had hurt her.," Calista told them, surprising Edward.

"When I told them they had strange smells, I had to explain the fact that I am a witch. She told me about them and about Jacob. I ended up questioning Bella's safety again, but they explained they meant her no harm.

But, he soon saw something on my wrist and explained who was causing all the local deaths.," She said.

Edward gently grabbed her wrist and placed a kiss upon the large, angry bruise. "I saw the bruise and connected things. The red-haired vampire causing the deaths, she had almost killed me. When Bella thought I was dead, she didn't want to live anymore. They had wanted to cause Bella extreme agony.," Calista said, leaning over to kiss the girl.

"Alice left the house, but soon came back with a single word, 'Edward!'. He thought Bella was dead, so he wanted to die too. We raced to save him, barely reaching him in time. He found out that I knew what he was, but our moment was soon cut short. The Volturi, the vampire government, wanted to see us.," She said, giving him a kiss.

"We were brought before them, surprising them with my presence. They tried to use their powers on Bella and decided that we needed to change or die. My hands became covered in black flames and I went to hurt them. Edward restrained me as Alice shared a vision with one of the leaders of us as vampires.," Calista admitted.

Her parents were taking this all very well. But, the Addams family was rather unusual themselves. Morticia had a pet carnivorous plant named Cleopatra. Cousin Itt was all hair! The Addams were used to the strange and different. They embraced the weird and dangerous things that surrounded them.

"You truly love them, Calista?," Morticia asked, staring into her eldest's blue eyes. She knew her daughter did, but she wanted to hear the words. "Yes, Mother. If they ever left, I would stop functioning and feed myself to Cleopatra! I love them with every fiber of my being and they return it.," Calista said, shocking her partners. She loved them, exactly as they loved her.

Gomez and Morticia shared a look before turning to Edward and Bella. "Welcome to the Addams Family! Excuse the crazy and the spooky. You make our daughter happy for the first time in her life. We thank you for that.," they told them. The love between the three was pure and true. "Calista, why don't you come officially meet my father tomorrow?," Bella asked.

Officially Meeting Mr. Swan

Bella arrived at the Addams house and waited for her girlfriend to come out. When she saw Calista, her breath hitched at how beautiful she looked. The girl could make a burlap sack work, she was perfect. Edward got out of the truck and opened the door for her. She gave him a quick kiss as thanks.

The car started on its journey to the Swan's, heading to see Charlie. Calista had met Bella's father before, but was nervous to be officially introduced. Their last meeting was when Bella was still depressed and now she was her girlfriend! Would he accept them? She knew he didn't like Edward, but not how he felt about her.

She had been so lost in thought and worry, oblivious they had reached the home. "He will love you, Cal.," Bella told her girlfriend, kissing her lips. Calista nodded, knowing she was being paranoid over nothing. Edward placed his hand on the small of her back as they walked toward the front door. Bella went in first, to announce she had something to tell Charlie.

The two of them entered, Edward rubbing circles on her spine in comfort. "Hello, Mr. Swan. I-I'm Bella's girlfriend. My name i-is Calista Addams.

You met me twice before. I'm the one who found her and I visited on my birthday.," Calista rambled out, blushing a deep red.

"I recognize you, Hun. I could tell from your reaction on the phone that you liked her. You seem to make her happy, so... Welcome to the Swans, Calista. Bells mentioned there was something else too.," Charlie told her, smiling at the girl.

"Thank you, sir. I'm also dating Edward... I fell for them both the day we met. I broke when I found out they were together, but here we are. They decided to allow me into their relationship. I love them both. If you can't accept him, then I don't want to be accepted either.," Calista told him, gaining confidence.

Charlie looked surprised; the girl was extremely blunt. His liking for her grew in that moment. He knew the two of them made Bella happy, but he hadn't expected this. "You've got spunk, Calista. I will try to accept him, but no promises. You have my support in this relationship.," He told her, surprising the three of them.

"Bella, you are grounded and HE isn't allowed in this house! You left, without a word!," Charlie told her, pointing at Edward when saying HE. The boy left the house, but she knew he would return later. "You have to get used to the fact that Edward is here to stay. Calista went with me too and her parents are still letting us see her!," Bella argued, silently signaling for her to go home.

Florida, Here We Come!

Little over a month later, Edward asks Charlie if he can take Bella to Florida. His parents had purchased two tickets and he said they would expire soon. They were also nonrefundable and another ticket had been bought to let Calista join them. Bella ended up fighting with her father and told him she could see her mother if she wanted to. Plus, she had not told her about Calista.

He reluctantly agreed, at least Calista would be there too. Three days later, the three lovers set off on a flight to Jacksonville, Florida. Calista became nervous, wondering why Bella had not told her mother yet. Was she embarrassed by her? The girl seemed to know what the other was thinking. "Cal, I just forgot. I love you, baby!," she told her, bringing her in for a deep kiss.

Calista nodded, she needed to stop being so paranoid. Bella and Edward loved her exactly as she did them. Soon, the plane landed and her girlfriend called her mother to come pick them up. Renee arrived with her ever so sunny disposition, causing Calista to smile. She could see where Bella got her smile.

Renee knew Edward, as she had met him when Bella was in the hospital. But, who was the pretty girl by their side? "Who's the beautiful girl, Bella?," she asked, blurting it out with no filter. Calista blushed as the woman complimented her. "Mom, this is our girlfriend, Calista Addams.," Bella told her.

"It's nice to meet you, Mrs. Dwyer! I absolutely love your daughter and Edward. I have since the moment I saw them. But, we started dating a little over a month ago. I promise that I will never hurt her.," Calista rambled.

The four of them got into Renee's car and drove to the house. She could tell that Calista would rather die before she hurt Bella. The three of them balanced each other out in the relationship. She had always liked Edward, while Charlie didn't. Bella started to talk to her mother as Calista played in the water.

Victoria and Powers

When the trio returned to school the next day, Jacob was there waiting for them. He tells Edward to keep his fellow 'leeches' oh their side of the treaty. This thoroughly confused the girls. Jake sees this and tells him off for keeping things from them. Emmett and Paul had clashed as they tried to get to Victoria.

Calista becomes enraged and takes off into the forest. She soon came to an empty clearing and decided to test her powers. Her hands once again become black flames, but she wants to see how far it will go. The flames began to climb up her arms and down her torso. In minutes, her entire body had been encased inside the onyx colored fire.

Those tickets could have been used anytime! Edward didn't want them here with Victoria around. The anger caused a blast of flame to hit one of the nearby trees. It immediately crackled and burned, turning black on contact. Soon, the tree disintegrated and ashes enveloped Calista's body.

She couldn't move or see anything around her. Her entire being began to burn as if her flames had consumed her. A tear slid down her cheek, but she still could not make a noise. Soon, Calista fell forward onto her knees, but she seemed to be alright. She stood up, but soon felt another power bubble to the surface.

She felt drawn to the location that had held the tree. Her feet led her to it and she knelt beside the empty spot. The soil seemed to beckon her, urging her to place her palm on it. Calista couldn't stop as her hand traveled to the dirt, running her fingers through it. An emerald green glow began to omit from it and into the ground.

Her body stood and backed up as the ground began to vibrate. Within seconds, a new tree erupted from the glowing soil, reaching the height of the others. A branch reached out to Calista and buried itself within her hand. She let out out a sharp gasp as the branch broke itself off underneath her skin. As she looked at the wound, it sealed up and a tingle spread through the area.

Soon, the wind began to pick up and lifted her off the ground. It carried her deeper into the forest and deposited her in the middle of a creek. The only thing the wind left behind was a small shiver down the back of her neck. Calista looked down at the water, which seemed to whirl around her feet. But, the water started to wrap around her leg and left a cold trail across her calf.

A crack was heard behind her, causing her to turn around. There stood Edward. He grabbed her from the creek and told her that school was over for the day. This confused her, how was school out already. Calista pulled out her phone and fainted, the time read 3 P.M. How had she lose the last 7 hours?!

Edward picked her up and carried her to the car, where Bella sat inside. He placed her in the backseat, buckling her up carefully. After arriving at the Cullen house, he carried her inside and laid her on the couch. "Carlisle! Something is wrong with Calista!," he called, panicking as she lay there in

Bella's lap. Instead of only Carlisle, the room was soon filled with the entire Cullen Coven, each with a look of worry.

Edward explained how she had reacted when she found out about Victoria. But, Calista had never returned from the forest, worrying him. He had to keep up appearances, so he remained until school was over. When he had found her, she was standing in the middle of a creek, only acknowledging him when the stick broke. He told her school was over and fainted when she realized.

Soon, a loud gasp was heard. Calista shot up on Bella's lap and soon a gust of wind whisked her to the nearest bathroom. Once inside, she stood and locked the door. Standing in front of a mirror, she removed her clothes and looked over her shoulder. She let out a sharp gasp at the sight before her.

Right between her shoulder blades was a new tattoo of a burning tree. She took a picture of it and then lifted her hair from her neck. There sat a tattoo of a blowing dandelion, which she documented as well. On her left calf, there was a wave, while there was a sprouting vine. The vine was located right where the branch had snapped beneath her skin.

Calista redressed and left the bathroom. Would she gain even more powers? She hoped she wouldn't lose a large expanse of time if she did. She sighed and walked into the living room. Everyone was still in the position they had been when she ran. "I-I know what happened now.," she said.

She pulled out her phone and shifted her stance. "I gained powers today. I had the one already, but didn't fully unlock until today. I was so angry, my whole body was enveloped in my black flames. A blast shot from my hand, burning and disintegrating a tree. Soon, the ashes consumed my body, which began to feel like it was burning. It left this mark on my back," Calista said, showing them the photo.

She breathed in and out as she recalled the events. "The spot where the tree was seemed to call to me. Before I knew it, I had my hand in the soil and it was glowing an emerald green. A new tree grew within seconds, but a branch reached out to me. It penetrated my arm and a section broke of inside. The wound closed itself right after and it left this mark.," Calista explained, showing them.

As she went on, it became easier to talk about. "Before I knew it, I was whisked away to the creek on a gust of wind. Apparently, that caused a mark of a blowing dandelion to appear on my neck. The wind dropped me in the middle of the creek. Water began to swirl around and soon climbed up my calf, leaving a cold trail. I guess it left this wave mark on my right leg. Edward founded me right after that.," Calista recalled, going to sit with her lovers.

Missing Things, A Bonfire, and Wednesday Addams

Two days later, Calista and Bella notice some things are missing in Bella's bedroom. She had left a couple dresses at the house, but now they weren't anywhere to be found. A pillow from the bed and a red blouse were also gone. Edward came over and detected an unfamiliar scent in the room. A strange vampire had been in the Swan house!

He brought them to the Cullen residence and they discussed who it could be. They had found a loophole in Alice's visions! Emmett and Jasper tracked the scent, but came back saying the vampire had left around two hours ago by car. Bella called Jacob to forgive him for saying she was better off dead than a vampire. Edward grabbed the phone and asks him to meet them at Bella's.

He has Jake watch the girls while he tries to track the scent. Jacob asks where the scent is strongest. He is taken aback when they tell him the strongest area is the bedroom, but soon catches the scent. He starts to question the relationship between Bella and Edward, focusing on when she is to be turned. When she tells him soon after graduation, his hand clenched around the knife in his hand.

Blood drops started falling to the kitchen tile and Bella rushes to clean it up. Calista was surprised at the news, Edward and Bella must have talked about it without her. She offers to bandage Jacob's hand, but he declined showing her the already healed cut. She begins to wonder if she actually is wanted in this relationship... Her girlfriend comes back over to them as she puts on a fake smile.

"Bella, do you want to come to a bonfire tonight? You can come too, Calista.," Jacob asks, adding her as an afterthought. Bella tells him she will have to ask if it's ok. "If we do go, can I bring my sister? I want to spend some time with her and get her out of the house.," Calista asks, receiving a nod from Jake. Edward chooses this moment to come back inside and the other boy heads back home.

Calista is good at hiding her emotions, so no one knows that she feels like an afterthought to everyone. Lately, she had started to feel unwanted in many places. Her parents focused more on Pugsley and Wednesday, barely acknowledging her existence. She thought that Edward and Bella would include her in things, but they too were pulling from her. She started to feel like she was a mistake to the people she loves.

Edward brings up Bella going to college, but she denies as she wants to be changed after graduation. She even mentions that waiting that long could be too risky. She asks him what Alice did with the stuff she was missing, but he said that she didn't take anything. He soon puts the pieces together, the intruder had taken the items as proof that she was found. Just as he picked up the phone to contact Carlisle, he received a call from him.

Carlisle tells him that things are getting worse in Seattle and something needed to be done. Edward decides to mention the bonfire and tells the girls to go. Calista heads home, crying silently as she entered her house. She knocks on Wednesday's door and wipes the tears away before the door opens. "I'm taking you to a bonfire, you need to meet people.," she said, grabbing the girl's wrist and pulling her to the car.

The girl broods the whole car ride there, but knows she needs to try and find friends. Calista looks at her in the rearview mirror and tells her that most of the people at the bonfire will be shifters. Wednesday becomes interested, mention the supernatural and you get her on the hook. She knows that her older sister is a witch who is dating a human and a vampire. The girls soon arrive at the location and exit the car.

Calista spots Bella, but her smile drops as she sees her beside Jacob. She drags Wednesday over to the people, becoming confused when her sister turns rigid. Looking up from the floor, she sees a young boy staring straight into her sister's eyes with a goofy smile. A young woman that looks a little like him slaps him on the back of the head. "Ow! Leah!," the boy whines.

Soon he walks over to the sisters and introduces himself. "Hi! I'm Seth. That's my older sister Leah. What are your names?," he asks, full of energy and bouncing. Calista smiles, he is so adorable, like a little puppy! "I'm Calista Addams and that's my little sister, Wednesday.," she tells him, pushing her sister. She stumbles, but Seth catches her.

Before Wednesday can recover and escape his arms, Calista runs to the other side of the clearing. The way Seth looked at her sister, she knew immediately that he had imprinted on her. He seemed like a great guy, but being a big sister, she would keep an eye out anyway. She sat down on the log and sighed. At least her sister now had happiness. Her eyes teared up as she looked at Jacob's arm around her girlfriend.

Soon, Billy Black, the boy's father, began to tell the stories of the tribe. Calista didn't know about this and felt like she was intruding, but calmed down as he looked straight at her. His fatherly gaze comforted her as her own father's did. He told them of how the tribe had started to shift, of the

Cold Ones attack. Another elder told the one that held her the most - the tale of the third wife's sacrifice.

The tribe had been decimated, the woman's old husband being the last shifter left. The damage had been caused by a female Cold One. She had attacked the tribe and the last shifter had to fight her. His wife, seeing the danger, stabbed herself in the stomach to distract her with the blood. Using the distraction, he was able to destroy the female. For a day, he remained with his dead wife in wolf form, before entering the forest and never returning.

Calista collected her sister, who wanted to return soon to see Seth. The two walked to the car and headed home. The entire bonfire Bella spent with Jacob. Her own girlfriend had ignored her! When they arrived home, the girls split ways and went to their beds. She laid herself down and cried herself to sleep.

Pain, Graduation, and Danger

T/W: mentions of self-harm

Calista spent the last week locked in her bedroom, but only Wednesday seemed to notice. She screamed at her older sister to open the door, but she wouldn't. She could smell the metallic scent of blood from outside the door. Running back to her room, she grabbed the axe from under her bed. She returned and destroyed the bedroom door.

The first thing that caught Wednesday's eye was the blood on the white marble floor. The next thing was Calista laying motionless on the bed. She screamed at the sight of her sister, sending her relatives running to the room. When Morticia entered the doorway, she dropped to her knees. Gomez held her as she screamed, her oldest child! Pugsley brushed his hand across his elder sister's cheek, jumping back as she let out a sharp gasp.

Calista sat up on the bed and saw her family surrounding her. She looked down at her arms, pouring blood as they had the entire week. Tears started to stream down her face as she realized what she had done. She had nearly ended her life at 18 and her sister had thought she found her body. Her body shook with heavy sobs.

"I-I'm so so-sorry! Things haven't been going well. Bella and Edward are making decisions without me and forgetting I exist. The same was happening here and I couldn't take it anymore.," Calista cried. She was the worst daughter ever!

The Addams family held her as she cried. They apologized, not having realized the pain they had put her through. Morticia told her that if she ever felt that way again to talk to them. Pugsley ran off and grabbed the first aid kit and Gomez bandaged her arms. Wednesday reminded her that today was the her graduation.

Her mother looked through her closet and picked out a dress and shoes. Calista called for Thing to come clean up the blood and she decided to make bracelets. She asked Grandmama to turn the razors in to fakes, but leave the blood stains. Tying string to them, Calista fastened them around her wrists. She wanted to remind herself to never do it again, representing the pain she had caused.

Wednesday helped Calista get dressed, but her sister decided to hug her. "Thank you.," she told her. After she was ready, they all packed into the car and drove to the school. Her graduation was here, but it seemed like it was only yesterday she had arrived. She took a deep breath and entered the school.

"Calista!! Where have you been, baby?!," shouted Bella Swan as she ran to the girl. Edward soon appeared by her side, frowning and tears that would never flow glistened in his eyes. He lightly grabbed her arms, pulling up her long sleeves. Her girlfriend started to cry as she saw the red-tinged bandages. "Why, Calista? Why did you do it, Lista?!," Edward whispered angrily.

"You were making decisions without me, forgetting I existed. It was only you and Bella! I thought you didn't love me anymore. My family was starting to forget about me. I-I couldn't take it!," Calista cried out, tears soaking her cheeks. Edward and Bella pulled their girlfriend into a hug, each kissing the top of her head.

"We're sorry, Love. We didn't mean to forget about you! The both of us love you, please don't ever do that again. If we lost you, we wouldn't know what to do. You complete us, baby. We have been planning something for you.," her partners told her.

The trio entered the gymnasium and waited to graduate. This was Bella and Calista's first high school graduation, causing them to be nervous. Edward had been through this too many times, giving him a calm demeanor. Soon, Calista's name was called and she received her diploma. Her partners applauding loudly as she did.

Edward's name was called not too long after and the girls cheered for him. It almost seemed to take forever for them to get to Bella's name, but when they did, Calista screamed her heart out. They had made it through together. After the graduation, the three headed to the Cullen's for their graduation party.

Bella told them of how she had connected everything and that the intruder was apart of the newborns. Calista couldn't believe she hadn't seen it before! Edward relayed this to his family, but soon the party was crashed by Jacob Black. He presented Bella with a charm bracelet, a handmade wolf charm hanging off. After accepting it, her girlfriend asked him if her right hook was too subtle of a uninvite.

Calista's eyebrow furrowed in confusion, but Edward filled her in. How dare he kiss her girlfriend?!! She walked over to him and grabbed his shirt collar, pulling him down to her level. "Kiss my girlfriend again and I will skin you, wolf-boy. I can also burn you alive if you prefer.," she growled at him, black flames dancing on her middle finger.

Edward and Bella pulled her away, rubbing circles on her back and kissing her neck. She soon calmed down, but smiled menacingly at the boy. Alice begins to have a vision, they aren't going to Seattle. The newborns are coming straight to them. The wolves present question this, asking what she's talking about. Edward tells them about the newborn army

Jacob wants the wolves to be involved. Alice sees what he means and thinks it is an excellent idea. "NO! Absolutely not!," Bella shouted, looking at Calista to back her up. She furiously shook her head as she thought of Edward, Leah, or Seth getting hurt. "You wanted us to get along, Bella. At least, we will still get to kill some vampires." Jake said. As much as the girls tried to protest, it was too late to stop them.

The wolves and the Cullens had decided to fight the newborns together. As they arranged to meet up in the forest at 3 A.M., Bella and Calista sat down on the steps and cuddled. Edward takes them to the Swan house and tries to get them to sleep. But, they insist on coming to the training to learn. Arriving at the clearing, Bella had a realization based on what had happened the year prior.

"Victoria! The newborns are her army! She wants us dead because you killed James...," Bella stated, causing their eyes to widen. At least there weren't separate groups wanting them dead. The wolves soon arrived and Jasper started the training. Calista walked to Seth's side and laid her head on him as Bella joined Jacob. After training, the wolves all leave, but he remains behind to talk to Edward.

Jacob has a great idea for him to mask the girls' scents. He suggests that Seth remain with them as a link between them and the pack. Edward surprisingly agrees with him for once! They create a plan together, getting along for once. The two part from one another on pleasant terms, remarking on the strange turn of events.

Gifts, Plans, and Engagements

Due to staying up, the girls have a late start to the day. Edward looks at Bella's bracelet and asks if he can be represented on it, a hand-me-down. He also tells her that they can't sneak down into the battle, but the girls retaliate. They either are down there in the battle, or he has to sit out with them. Edward chooses to sit out with them, they are his world and cannot bear to lose them.

Soon, he leaves to go talk strategy with Jasper. As he leaves, Alice comes to replace him. When Charlie comes home, she tells him that tomorrow and Friday the others would be camping. This would leave her all alone in that big house, tricking him into suggesting Bella join her. Calista sends a quick text to her parents letting them know she would be staying at the Cullens too.

Soon, it is time for the girls to go to bed, Edward waiting in there for them. Instead of Alice, he would be staying there with them all alone on tomorrow night! Bella and Calista share a look as they become excited at being alone with him. Soon, they head off to the clearing to watch the training. The girls feel guilty when the realize that the group would still be outnumbered.

The next night, Calista and Bella arrive at the Cullen house. They are nervous as they kiss Edward, the same thought in their heads. The girls want to be with him before they are changed. Calista kisses his neck as Bella talks. "I want you before I'm turned. It seems Calista does too.," she says, confusing him.

Her hands start unbuttoning his shirt as the other girl tries to nibble on his ear. Realizing what they are trying to do, Edward grabs Bella's wrists and pulls Calista in front of him. "Girls, I can't. Not while you are human, I'll hurt you!," he cries, hardly resisting them. They look at him pleadingly and ask him to at least try. An idea pops into his head and telling them he would try after they were married.

The mention of marriage sent Calista's heart fluttering, her eyes darting to her bag. She crept off the bed and grabbed the bag, nerves causing her stomach to do flips. At the same time, Edward reached into the bedside table and removed two things. He opens a box and shows his mother's ring to Bella. Having her slide it on her finger, he kneels down in front of them.

"Isabella Marie Swan, will you do me the honor of becoming my wife?," Edward asks. In spite of the reluctance she held, she agreed to become his wife. Soon, he turns to Calista and opens the second box. Laying inside the box was a black ring with a mystic topaz gem. "Calista Ophelia Addams, will you do me the honor of becoming my wiccan wife?," he asks, a tear trailing down her cheek. She furiously nods before pulling him into a kiss.

Edward tells her that finding the ring had occupied a lot of his time, but he had help. Her parents had been there with him, aiding him in the search. Smiling, she asks him to sit on the bed with Bella. He followed her instructions as she took his place on the floor. She takes a deep breath before grabbing one of the boxes.

"Edward Masen Cullen, you stole half of my heart the moment we met. The first time we kissed, you returned it to me, but to this day you still own it. This ring symbolizes how without you, I could not live. Will you do me the honor of becoming my undead husband?," Calista asks, laughing at her proposal.

He nods and lets her slip the ring on his finger, giving her a small peck. "Bella, when I thought I lost you, I wanted to die beside you. The other half of my heart belongs to you. This ring symbolizes your beauty to me, the black rose is rare and gorgeous. Will you become my wife?," Calista asks, staring into her chocolate eyes. Bella nods, sliding on the ring as she kisses her.

"This honestly wasn't planned, but I don't want to feel left out!," Bella says, laughing as she pulls out two rings. The three laugh, they were all proposing on the same night! "Edward, I love you. Carlisle told me your eyes were green as a human. The gems in this ring will be a reminder of who you were and are. Marry me?," she asks, sliding the ring on his finger as he nods.

"Calista, you are unique. Your heart contains love for the both of us and I love it. This ring took a lot of time to pick, but your parents helped me out. Marry me, Cal?," Bella asks. The ring was the silver triple moon, a gem sitting in the middle. The gem was a dragon's breath fire opal, a perfect companion to the mystic topaz. She nodded and allowed her to slip on the ring. The three of them enjoy the rest of the night in each other's company.

The Fight, Bree, and Saving them

The morning of the battle, Edward asks Bella why she isn't wearing her rings. Jacob overhears this and runs off, Bella following. Calista looks at Edward, before reentering the tent to get ready. She puts on some face paint that Grandmama said would help bring luck to them. Reaching into her bag, she grabs a dagger and slides it up her sleeve.

Calista had remembered the tale of the third wife's sacrifice and came prepared to protect those she loves. Soon, Bella comes back with a guilty look upon her face. She tells them that Jacob had gone to the battlefield. Soon, Edward tells them that the battle has finally begun. His head snaps over to the tent opening, rushing outside.

"Seth, run!," Edward yells and the boy hides. The girls exit the tent just as Riley and Victoria approach. He tells Riley that she is using him, she didn't really love him. Her true mate had been killed by Edward and she wanted him to pay. She whispered in his ear that she had warned him of their tricks.

Riley lunges toward them, but Seth attacks him. Edward starts to fight Victoria, but the wolf is soon launched into a tree. This leaves their fiancé to fend for himself. Bella reaches for a rock, but Calista knocks it from her hand. She reaches up her sleeve and grabs the dagger.

Calista rolls up her sleeve, presenting the pale flesh to the world. Before anyone can react, she slashes the blade across her arm violently. Crimson blood begins to drip onto the ivory snow below. The scent distracting Riley and Victoria, who try and lunge for her. This allows Seth to tear Riley apart, while Edward beheads the woman.

Once dismembered, Calista sets them alight with her black flames. Edward rushes to her side and tries to stop the dripping blood. She pulls away and shows him her arm. While it is covered in blood, there is no longer a wound. "Grandmama taught me that a couple days ago. I wanted to protect you.," she tells him.

"Never do that again, Lista!," Edward yells before pulling her in for a deep kiss. Suddenly, Seth lets out an agonizing whine, but he isn't the one hurt. They rush to the battlefield where Jacob Black lays hurt, the left side of his body broken. Carlisle tells the wolves to bring the boy home and he would come over to rebreak his bones correctly. Beside Jasper stands a newborn in pain due to the girls presence.

As Calista looks at her, she feels an immediate connection. It was the same feeling she had when meeting Seth. She had to protect this girl, having a hunch that she would be Pugsley's mate. A moment later, the Volturi entered the clearing and approached. Edward explained that they had destroyed the newborn army.

"You missed one.," Jane stated, her red eyes staring at the girl. Carlisle told her that she had surrendered and deserved a second chance. The female guard said they didn't give second chance and order Felix to dispose of her. Calista growled, her body setting alight. "Over my dead body, bitch! Touch her and you will be ashes.," she said, the Cullens surrounding the newborn.

"Very well, master won't be pleased they are still human.," Jane said, backing away from Calista. One of the most feared vampires was afraid of her! "The date has been set!," Alice chimed. This was news to her. The Volturi nodded and left them in the clearing.

"What's your name, honey?," Calista asked the girl. She appeared to be barely older than Pugsley! "Bree. Bree Tanner.," she replied staring at her feet. Looking up at the older girl, she soon felt safe and no longer wanted to bring her harm. "Well, Bree, I think I might know your mate.," Calista told her.

Pugsley's Happiness

The day before her wedding, Calista decided to bring Bree to meet Pugsley. She had been watching the young vampire with Carlisle and found she had an extreme amount of control. On the car ride to the Addams house, she watched the girl's body language. She had chosen to sit in the back seat and fidgeting nervously, one human habit that she retained. "It's ok, Bree. Pugsley is going to fall head over heels for you!," she told the girl, smiling at her in the rearview mirror.

The brunette girl nodded and calmed down. When the car stopped in front of the Addams house, Calista grabbed Bree's shoulder and led her inside. "Pugsley! Where are you? I have surprise in the living room!," she called out as they stood at the bottom of the stairs. At the sound of his name, the boy ran to the stairs and raced down them.

His foot missed the next step and he tumbled down, landing at the girls' feet. Calista grabbed her brothers hand, hauling him up and brushing him off. "Pugsley, this is Bree. If my intuition is correct, the two of you are mates.," she told him, causing him to look up. Eyes scanning over the girl, he gasped at her beauty.

Bree Tanner had beautiful and flawless porcelain skin, reminding him of an angel. Her eyes were a mixture of red and gold, signifying her change in diet, but they captured his heart. The hair upon her head was a dark brown, completing her perfection. Pugsley Addams was speechless at the sight of the gorgeous girl. "Wow! You're so pretty!," he spouted.

As Calista looked at Bree, she smiled as the girl stared at her brother in awe. The Addams siblings had now all found their mates. Pugsley had Bree to spend his life with now. Wednesday had Seth Clearwater, a shapeshifter who would rather die than allow harm to her. Finally, she had Edward and Bella, who she would cherish for eternity.

Their eternity would start tomorrow!

Getting Married to Forever

The day had actually arrived! Today, Calista was to marry Edward and Bella. This would be the first day of their forever! As she pulled up to the Cullen's house, Rosalie stood there waiting for her. She told her which room to go to and the wind carried her there.

The blonde pulled Calista out of the way as Alice came rushing into the room. "I just left Bella looking perfect, but now it's your turn!," the pixie enthused. She locked the door before thrusting a garment bag into the bride's hands. They helped her into the dress before handing her two garters. A throat cleared outside the door and a knock followed.

Rosalie opened the door to reveal Morticia and Gomez Addams. She left to go tend to the guests and sit at the piano. "This was mine when I married your father.," her mother said as she revealed a crown. At the same time, he pulled out a veil and told her she was borrowing it. Alice attached the two items together before placing them on Calista's head. Soon, she slipped on her heels and it was time.

Calista froze up, realizing that she was about to be married! Gomez placed his hand on her shoulder and told her it would be alright. Alice told them that Bella was now at the end of the aisle with Edward, waiting for her to join them. Her father led her down the staircase and out the back door. Wrapping an arm around her waist, he began to walk her down the aisle.

At the altar stood Edward dressed in a sexy black tuxedo and across from him stood Bella. She was wearing a dress inspired by the 1900s but with a modern train and veil. Calista's heart fluttered at the sight of them. She wore a black dress with lace sleeves, the neckline showing off her cleavage a bit. The view of her left her lovers awed by her beauty. Gomez walked her to her future husband and wife, giving her over to them.

The priest began the ceremony and the three lovers stared into each other's eyes. Soon it was time for the exchanging of the rings. Each had paired together to pick out the rings. Edward slipped the moonstone ring on the brunette's left ring finger. Calista slid the white gold band upon his hand. Finally, Bella placed the opal ring upon her finger.

"I now pronounce you married. You may now kiss each other!," shouted the priest. Edward kissed each girl deeply, before they kissed each other. They were now the Cullens. Soon, the newlyweds were directed to a table as speeches began. Jessica's rather annoyed the brides, you couldn't have him- get over it he's married now! Before long it was time for the father-daughter dance.

After Bella had danced with Charlie, Gomez approached Calista. Their eyes connected and they nodded before turning to the rest of the Addams family. As the signal was given, he led her to the middle of the floor. Within the blink of an eye, the family had each produced an instrument. The music was that of a tango as they began to play.

A/N: play the video now and imagine whatever you want for the dance

After finishing the dance, Gomez goes to return Calista to her husband and wife. But Rosalie whisks her away into the house as Alice takes Bella upstairs. Arriving in the room she shares with Emmett, Rose helps the girl out of her dress and removes her crown and veil. She puts on the red and black dress and heads to the living room. Bella and Edward are waiting for her there, kissing her sweetly as she joins them. The married trio runs toward the car as the guest pelt them with rice, heading toward their honeymoon.

Honeymoon: Night 1

A/N: please excuse my attempt at sexy times

Right after the reception, the newly wedded trio start to head to their honeymoon. But, their destination isn't reached until the next night! Edward steers the boat to a dock at a beautiful island and tells them this is it. The girls eyes widen as they realized it would just be them on this island. "This is Isle Esme. Carlisle gifted to her as a wedding present. They decided to lend it to us for our honeymoon.," he explained.

When they reached the house, Edward swept the girls up in his arms and carried them across the threshold. Once inside, he told them he would be in the ocean waiting for them. He wanted to the give them a 'human moment' as he called it, to freshen up. Holding hands, the girls entered the bathroom.

Calista grabbed a razor and shaving cream before lathering up their legs. Using a steady hand, she started to shave Bella, who in turn did the same. Once they had finished their legs, they shaved the rest of their bodies. As they wrapped each other in towels, they leaned in and shared a deep and passionate kiss. Holding hands, Calista led her wife outside.

The sight that met them was Edward's bare back, illuminated by the beautiful moonlight. With a nod, Bella and Calista dropped their towels and walked into the water. The brunette placed herself against his side while the redhead moved in front. The girls began to kiss his lips and neck, hands roaming over his flawless skin. He let out a low growl, each hand starting to squeeze his wives hips.

A/N: My attempt at smut starts here

Before the girls could realize it, Edward had whisked them back into the house. He tossed them down onto the bed and gazed at their naked bodies. His eyes were black with a hunger, but it wasn't blood he needed. Calista began to run her hand over Bella's stomach and down to her thigh, giving a small squeeze. The brunette gasped and tried to lower the hand.

Edward crouched over them and ran his finger across the redhead's lips. She slipped his finger into her mouth, sucking on it as she stared into his eyes. Her hand moved between Bella's legs, dancing over her lower lips before slipping a finger in. The girl let out a moan, rocking herself on her wife's finger. Their husband lowered his head to Calista's chest, nibbling upon her pierced nipples.

She grabbed his hair and asked him to remove his mouth, she wanted to try something else. Calista spread Bella's legs open, revealing her vagina and lowered her mouth to it. Her tongue flicked against her wife's clit, savoring her sweet juices. Edward couldn't take it as her own vagina glistened at him. He lifted her lower half and began to devour her folds.

The three let out moans, the girls soon reaching their first orgasm of the night. Parting, Calista grabbed his penis, licking the tip as Bella played with his balls. She lowered her mouth and took him into the back of her throat, bobbing her head. Soon, she pulled away and Bella took her place, but gagged as she tried to take him in. Edward growled and pushed them back down onto the bed.

He grabbed Calista and rubbed his tip against her glistening slit, looking into her eyes. As she nodded, he pushed in, taking her virginity as she moaned. Bella knelt beside the bed, kissing her wife as their husband made love to her. His pace increased as his hands wrapped around her throat, grunting as he got closer. Soon, he erupted inside her as she orgasmed twice.

Edward stood up and Calista moved to beside the bed. As Bella took her place, she began to question what had just happened. Did her husband, a vampire, just ejaculate?! She shook her head, thinking her mind must be playing tricks on her. Soon, her wife orgasmed as she kissed her lips. The night continued like this, until the girls passed out.

Honeymoon: Unexpected Results

----

2 weeks had passed since the trio started their honeymoon. But, things weren't going as planned. Calista hadn't opened her eyes since the first night! Edward and Bella were scared for their wife. The only thing they knew was that she was alive, seeing her chest rise and fall. They had called Carlisle at least six times, but even he was clueless.

When Calista had fallen into her state, Bella had strange dreams and a change in her appetite. Edward had gone to hunt, knowing that they would be safe. Realizing that her period had not come, she rushed to the bathroom and lifted her shirt. There sat a small bump, she was pregnant! If she was, could Calista be too?

When Edward returned, Bella told him of her pregnancy and her speculation about their wife. Calling Carlisle, he announced that they were returning and he needed to check on the girls. She passes him one of Calista's dresses and he puts it on her carefully. As he leaves to take their bags to the boat, she calls Rosalie and begs her to help keep the baby. She hides the phone as he returns to take them back to Forks.

Little did they know that Calista had a bump that was twice the size of Bella's.

A/N: Calista wakes up when one of the Cullens touch her

Pregnancy and Labor

When Calista woke from her long slumber, the first thing she did was cradle her stomach. It was mother's instinct, immediately knowing of her children. She had regained consciousness when Esme had caressed her cheek. The woman jumped back and screamed as the blue eyes popped open. Carlisle, Bella, and Edward ran into the room, surprised by the sight before them.

"You aren't going to hurt my sunshines! I would never forgive you!," Calista screamed as she cradled her bump. Suddenly everyone else faded away, leaving her, her children, and Bella's baby. Her sanity began to deteriorate as she sang about them. As she sang, Carlisle called Morticia and Gomez to come over.

A/N: Play the video here

As her parents entered the house, they caught sight of her curled on the floor. She was rubbing her stomach with a blank look and singing repeatedly. Their daughter had been gone for two weeks and now looks about halfway through a pregnancy! Tears began to trail down Morticia's cheeks and a sob forced its way from her lips. At the sound, Calista snapped out of it and looked at them.

"Mommy! Daddy! Don't let them take my sunshines, none of them!," she pleaded and walked over in front of Bella. She lifted her wife's shirt and placed kisses upon the small bump. Calista had three sunshines waiting to enter the world and would not allow harm to come to them. The brunette wouldn't let anything happen if something went wrong.

Morticia and Gomez kissed their daughter's cheek and drove home sobbing. They couldn't lose her!

Time skip to a week later

Jacob Black stormed into the Cullen house, demanding to see Bella. "Jacob, it's best if you don't come in.," Carlisle told the boy, but stopped when she called for him. He entered, seeing the entire Cullen family surrounding her and Calista. The girls were sitting on the couch as he approached. Rosalie was protecting them and they were comforting an upset Edward.

The two women stood up, their pregnant bellies being revealed to Jake. He recoiled at the sight of something that shouldn't have been possible! Edward demanded to see him outside and confirmed that they were dying. He was slowly killing his wives and wanted to get rid of what was hurting them. Bella and Calista wouldn't allow anything to happen, even as they were drained of life.

Edward offered him to give the girls what they wanted, just to save them. Jake attempts to change their minds, but they remained the same. Bella and Calista would keep their hearts beating until these children were born. After leaving he phased and the situation was revealed to the pack. When they wanted to kill the girls, he left the pack and formed his own in their protection. Seth and Leah followed him, the former want to protect his girlfriend's sister.

Time skip to the week of birth

Jacob entered the room with Edward and Rosalie wanted them to listen to the girls out of their baby names. "If it is a boy, I like E.J. for Edward Jacob.," Bell told them. The blonde said that wasn't too bad, but to try and persuade her from the girl name. "If it is a girl, I choose... Reneesme. Combining Esme and Renee. I mixed Charlie and Carlisle to make Carlie for the middle name.," she said. The Quileute boy told her he liked it.

Rosalie gestured for Calista to tell them the names she had picked, even she didn't know them yet. The redhead was sure that the twins were a boy and a girl. "For the girl, I mixed Rosalie and Emmett's names for the first name, Emmalie. For the middle name, I mixed Wednesday and Bree's names to make Wren.," she told them. If the blonde could cry, tears would be flowing. The name was beautiful!

"For the boy, I mixed Alice and Jasper's names to make Jace. I tried mixing Pugsley and Seth, but couldn't come up with anything good. I decided to go with Lee. I wanted to include our siblings because Bella chose our parents. Plus, my parents names aren't exactly combinable.," Calista told them.

Soon, it was time for the girls to drink some blood, the only thing the babies wanted. As Rosalie handed them the Styrofoam cups, Bella's fell out of her hand. She bent to grab it before it could hit the floor, but screamed out as her spine snapped. Calista crumbled to the floor beside the blood, falling on her back. Each twin had reacted to the brunette's screams with a kick to their mother's spine. One hit the top and the other the bottom, completely disconnecting her spine from her frame.

Both women went into labor, fighting for their lives.

Babies, Transformations, and Death?!

The girls were carried upstairs and placed on two tables. Bella screamed for them to save baby and Rosalie sliced her stomach. At the sight of the blood, the blonde was transfixed and dragged out of the room. Soon the sound of teeth penetrating hard flesh was heard and followed by the cry of an infant. "It's Renesmee!," Edward tells her as he hands her the child. The child bites her mother and the brunette's heart starts to fade out.

He offers Renesmee to Jacob, but he curtly told him to throw her out the window. Rosalie takes the baby instead and Edward injects his venom into Bella's heart. Soon, the Quileute realized he still felt the pull, but its source had now changed. He followed the pull, obeying it by his own choice. His eyes connected with the child's and his universe now revolved around her. He had imprinted on the child!

A scream of anguish was heard from the table beside Bella. Calista couldn't move but had just saw her wife die! Her eyelids began to flutter as she muttered for Edward to save the twins. The first to enter the world was Emmalie. Alice entered and took her, waiting to take Jace as well. Once he was delivered, Edward looked up at the redhead. The sight that awaited him was her lifeless blue eyes, staring at nothing.

A/N: The song above was going through her head as she died

Edward set to injecting Calista with his venom before leaving the room. He heard a noise outside of the house and found Esme, Carlisle, and Emmett being attacked by the Uley Pack. He tells them that the girls didn't make it. Jacob runs out of the house and tells them they can't harm the children. "You can't harm an imprint and I won't let you hurt the twins either!," he yells, surprising everyone.

Three-day jump, when Bella wakes

Over the past three days, Bella's body had repaired itself and she was about to wake up. Alice didn't see Calista waking up and her body had remained broken! None of them could bear to lose her, especially not the twins and Renesmee. Edward started to wonder if he had been too late for her and slid himself onto the floor. At that moment, Bella's eyes snapped open and took in the new view.

Bella heard Edward make contact with the floor and followed his gaze. She saw Calista's prone form laying still and broken on the table beside her. "NO! Cali! Why isn't she changed?!," she screamed as her eyes filled with venom tears.

Little did they know Calista could hear everything.

I'm Coming Home

While Edward was taking Bella out on her first hunt, Alice Cullen had a vision! She gasped as the vision played out, shocked at what it showed. Calista Cullen was not dead! An internal war was being waged inside the redheaded woman.

Inside the woman screamed, wanting to reunite with her spouses and their three children! But something was restraining her, holding her in the darkness of unconsciousness. She saw flashes of color: a crimson red against a beautiful blue. The two colors fought almost destroying one another before a third and fourth appeared. A beautiful golden topaz entertwined with a chocolate brown reached out and drew the fighters together, combining them as one.

Calista's broken and lifeless body started to mend itself. The redhead began to stir, soon she would be waking up. Her body was beautiful once more, her piercings, scars, and tattoos remaining. For she wasn't only a vampire, she was still a witch. This was the moment Alice flitted downstairs, collecting the woman's returning spouses from the yard.

As Bella and Edward entered the room, Calista shot up and her eyes opened. Revealing her new hybrid eyes.

(Alice had hid her thoughts as Bella fought with Jake, more interesting twists to come)

Panic Room

Right after Calista woke up

"Where are the kids?!," she gasped and started to try to find them, only to be restrained by her spouses. This shocked the redhead, did they think she was going to hurt them? She looked up at them with a face that showed her feelings, that she was betrayed by them. In the next moment, Calista had broken out of their grasps and opened the window. She turned back to them with a small snarl before jumping out and taking off.

Her feet took a path of their own, leading her to a very familiar location. Before her stood, the Addams family mansion in the woods, where she had lived. Calista knocked on the door and soon Lurch opened it. With a gust of wind, she darted into the home and toward her parents, tears falling as she sobbed noiselessly. Gomez and Morticia were shocked, having heard that their daughter didn't change when Bella did.

"What's wrong, Mi Amor?," they asked as they held her, seeing her two different colored eyes. "E-Edward and Bella, they thought I would hurt our little sunshines! I-it hurt so much, I ran and ended up here.," Calista sobbed. Morticia explained that the redhead would need to tell her loves of the hurt and return after changing clothes. She handed her an outfit, the one they had planned to bury her in and sent her to change before going to Grandmama.

The old witch handed her a large flask and told her to make the redhead drink it. She had never revealed to the family that she had known that Calista would become the hybrid she now is. The flask was full of blood, some from each witch of the girl's bloodline. This would keep her fed for over a century, before she would need to drink again.

When handed the flask, the redhead knew not to refuse and drank it fast. "Now, return to them, Mi Amor!," Gomez said and placed a kiss on her head. She sped out with a nod, her feet carrying her back to her heart. Her steps weren't heard as she entered, spotting Edward and Bella cradling 3 figures. But as her approach got closer, she could see them clearly. "Who are you holding? Where are our sunshines?," she asked frantically.

"Calista! These are Renesmee, Jace, and Emmalie.," Edward said calmly. But the redhead shook her head. "No! Where are they?!," she cried, but they stepped closer. The three children reached for her and she broke. "N-no... T-they are only 3 days old!," she sobbed as she clutched her head. At this moment, 4 sets of footsteps along with the scent of wolf reached Calista.

"Is Cal- oh. We have something to tell you.," three of the wolves said. It was Embry Call, Jacob Black, and Leah Clearwater. Seth stood beside them in a sling. "Rose! Come get the kids!," Bella called and soon they were whisked to another room. "What's going on?," the redhead asked. Edward led them all outside, saying it would be best for this to be told there. Calista started to panic even more.

"Seth, I'm still sorry...," Bella said, making him chuckle. "No big deal just don't do it again or Calista might not like it.," he said. This confused the redhead to no end. "What happened? How did he get hurt?," She asked, demanding answers. The only one she received was that there had been a misunderstanding.

"C-Calista, we can't help when it happens...," Jacob began. "I-It's something we can't control...," continued Embry. "I-I didn't think it could happen...," finished Leah. With those words for Leah, everything clicked together and something snapped within her. "Y-you... imprinted on my children?," she stuttered staring at her feet, her body twitching slightly.

In response, she received 3 answers of yes, finding that she had taken it much better than Bella. Within the blink of an eye, Calista's head shot up, revealing pitch black eyes and veins surrounding them. Her hands emitting a black smoke as they shot out, causing the three wolves to raise into the air. Each gasped for air, clutching at their throats as a demented smile began to form on the redheads face. She began to sing the song "Panic Room", but it sounded demented - almost like it wasn't her.

But just as she started the chorus, the woman's eyes rolled back into her head and she screamed. The scream was horrific as her body fell to the ground and thrashed, black leaking from her eye sockets as they squeezed tightly shut. The wolves fell to the ground as well, as the black smoke in her hands disappeared. Everyone knew that Calista wouldn't have done that, so what had happened? Was this a new power that couldn't be controlled or had something possessed her?

Meet the Frumps

Now, you are probably wondering why this side of my family had been introduced earlier! The answer is that they lived halfway across the world. Now It's time to meet the 4 Frump women:

The matriarch of the family is Ophelia Frump. She is the sister of Morticia Addams.

She had triplet daughters, who turned out to all be witches:

The eldest, Eris Morticia Frump, has a power over the shadows, the dead, and ghosts:

The middle triplet, Ariadne Umbra Frump, has power over spiders and is clairvoyant:

The youngest triplet, Pythia Diana Frump, has cosmic powers and the power to shapeshift:

Not Feeling Myself

Calista's body was extremely still, as lifeless as prior to her change. Her bizarre, hybrid heart could no longer be heard, causing panic within those around her. The Addams family had just entered the backyard at the start of the panic. No one knew what had happened or what would. They all had but one thought: Had this new power or some kind of possession ended her life?

Inside the mother of three, another internal war started. However unlike with her change, the war was NOT with herself. While she appeared lifeless on the outside, her mind had created what appeared to be a battlefield. Her eyes tried to see the other side, but a thick fog coated the area before her. Calista looked down and gasped at her attire, a mirror showing her appearance.

Eventually the fog parted to reveal a path and a hooded figure at the other end. What scared her was that with every step on the path, the figure copied. Soon the two stood in front of one another, hooded and faceless to each other. With shaking hands, Calista grasped her hood and pulled it down. Knowing that the figure had done the same, she slowed looked up and did a double take.

The woman's eyes shot open as Calista examined their similarities. Pitch black stared into red and blue, a sinister smirk appearing on the former's face. A familiar tune was hummed, causing her to realize what was going on. "It was you! You made me hurt them! Why? Who are you?!," she rambled. Her hands lit up with her black fire in anger.

The black-eyed woman's smirk dropped, and she snapped her fingers. This small action forced Calista to her knees, unable to get up. Her chin was roughly gripped in the woman's hand, forcing her to look her in the face. "Learn your place, girl! Is that anyway to talk to the reason you are alive? Without me, you wouldn't have those powers you covet. I'm known as Valdis, but you can refer to me as Ancestor or Coven Leader.," she spat.

An intense pain flooded Calista's body, making her let out a scream. In reality, everyone watched in horror as her top became coated in blood. Looking down on the battlefield, she saw the same blood. "Why Ancestor? What did I do for your wrath?," she asked softly, bloody tears trailing down her cheeks. No words were spoken as Valdis brushed her hand on her cheek.

"Hush, My child. The time has come for our line to have a new Coven Leader. I have decided that it shall be you, Calista Ophelia Addams Cullen. For your heart is one of a leader. That of a selfless woman who would dare to face anything for those she cares about, no matter the consequences. Who loves with her entire being and senses her people.," the woman explained.

Valdis released Calista's chin and pulled her to her feet, putting her hand on the woman's chest. In reality, a multicolored light emitted from the spot before fading. "I wanted to protect your family, but now I sense that I shouldn't have intervened. Do give my apologize to them. However, it might have been the only way to bring you here. The place I sacrificed my life to save our line. I'll be seeing you soon, dear.," she whispered and snapped her fingers. At that moment, Calista's eyes opened and she gasped for air.

www.ingramcontent.com/pod-product-compliance
Lightning Source LLC
Chambersburg PA
CBHW071026080526
44587CB00015B/2526